Department of the Treasury
Alcohol and Tobacco Tax and Trade Bureau

Strategic Plan

Fiscal Years 2007–2012

Department of the Treasury
Alcohol and Tobacco Tax and Trade Bureau

STRATEGIC PLAN

Fiscal Years 2007–2012

Table of Contents

Challenging times call for leaders who can, and will, meet the challenges of today—and tomorrow. Seeking a vision beyond the current domain of business as usual is imperative. The learning curve has never been steeper, the resources never tighter, and the ingenuity to collect the revenue that is rightfully due while protecting the public on a number of fronts has never been more important.

Since the founding of the Republic, TTB's mission to collect the revenue has helped sustain the economy and provide economic stability. Increasing technological advances have helped relieve the tax burden for many industry members. TTB has also reduced the tax burden for small businesses by instituting fewer reporting requirements. TTB is writing regulations in plain language to provide a greater probability of compliance. Significant TTB resources have been allocated to educate our industry members as a preferred action to enforcement.

This educational culture carries over into TTB's Protect the Public programs where TTB inculcates a spirit of public service integrity in its employees and a character of business integrity, product integrity, and market integrity in the industry members for the commodities it regulates. The workforce engages in leading edge training that requires interaction with other agencies to assure that best practices are the norm and that resources are used most effectively and efficiently.

These are not just words but a daily creed for TTB's men and women who adhere to a common cause—collect the revenue that is rightfully due and protect the public from dangerous or misleading alcohol beverage and tobacco products through industry education efforts, and where necessary, enforcement actions.

The way we do business is constantly changing, therefore the need for continuous strategizing and long-term comprehensive strategic planning is greater than ever. TTB strives to clearly define, and occasionally redefine, its goals within the mission; TTB must implement strategic thinking and planning to facilitate those efforts. With each update to the TTB Strategic Plan, our resolve grows stronger. This Plan and its predecessors provide clear guidance to help us better protect and serve the public and to ensure that the regulated industries comply with the law.

TTB Administrator
John J. Manfreda

Secretary of the Treasury John Snow appointed John J. Manfreda as the Administrator of the Alcohol and Tobacco Tax and Trade Bureau (TTB), effective January 4, 2005. Mr. Manfreda, served as Deputy Administrator of TTB since the Bureau's founding in January 2003.

As Administrator, Mr. Manfreda oversees the collection of nearly $15 billion per year in Federal alcohol, tobacco, firearms and ammunition excise taxes, as well as the permit systems and regulations established for those industries under the authority of the Internal Revenue Code and the Federal Alcohol Administration Act.

As TTB moves forward, the organization is ever-mindful of integrating our performance measures, budget, and strategic planning. TTB must manage for results today with an eye always on the future. TTB continues to forge a path that ensures we can achieve our mission, make our vision a reality, and administer our programs effectively and efficiently.

This Plan sets forth the guidelines that TTB needs to serve the public. I am proud of this Plan and the employees who work so diligently toward achieving our goals.

John J. Manfreda

Administrator

TTB History. On November 25, 2002, President George W. Bush signed into law the Homeland Security Act of 2002. One provision of this Act abolished the Bureau of Alcohol, Tobacco and Firearms (ATF) and created two new bureaus, the Bureau of Alcohol, Tobacco, Firearms and Explosives, which moved to the Department of Justice, and the Alcohol and Tobacco Tax and Trade Bureau (TTB), which remained in the Department of the Treasury.

The TTB mission and its predecessor agencies date back to the creation of the Treasury Department and the first Federal taxes levied on distilled spirits in 1791.

TTB Responsibilities. TTB administers and enforces the Federal laws and implements regulations related to the production and taxation of alcohol and tobacco products, as well as the statutes that impose Federal excise tax on firearms and ammunition.

The major responsibilities of TTB include:

- Administering the laws that govern alcohol, tobacco, firearms, and ammunition excise taxes and classifying alcohol and tobacco products for excise tax purposes.

- Investigating applications and issuing permits or notices for the operation of distilleries, bonded wine premises, and breweries.

- Investigating applications and issuing permits for manufacturers, importers, and export warehouse proprietors of tobacco products.

- Regulating the operations of various industrial users of distilled spirits, including manufacturers of non-beverage products, and tax-free and denatured alcohols.

- Collecting firearms and ammunition excise taxes.

- Regulating the production, packaging, and storage of alcohol and tobacco products and labeling and bottling of alcohol beverages.

- Ensuring that labeling and advertising of alcohol beverages provide adequate information to the consumer concerning the identity of the product.

- Preventing misleading labeling or advertising of alcohol beverages.

- Regulating the marketing and promotional practices concerning the sale of alcohol beverages by producers, importers, and wholesalers primarily through the investigation of allegations of unfair trade practices.

- Enforcing provisions of the Alcoholic Beverage Labeling Act, which mandates that a Government warning statement appear on all alcohol beverages for sale and distribution in the United States.

- Briefing members of Congress and Treasury officials on matters relating to alcohol beverages, tobacco products, and firearms and ammunition excise taxes.

Vision, Mission, and Values

Vision

Our vision is to be an organization of people who value each other and who treat each other and their customers with the respect that they deserve. TTB intends to uphold the laws, for which TTB is responsible, in a fair and practical way, affording all an opportunity to have public opinions heard without prejudice. TTB intends to carry out its missions without imposing inappropriate or undue burden on those from which TTB collects taxes and those TTB regulates.

Mission

The mission of TTB is to:

- Collect alcohol, tobacco, firearms, and ammunition excise taxes that are rightfully due;

- Protect the consumer of alcohol beverages through compliance programs that are based upon education and enforcement of the industry to ensure an effectively regulated marketplace; and

- Assist industry members to understand and comply with Federal tax, product, and marketing requirements associated with the commodities we regulate.

Values

TTB employees value each other and those TTB serves. TTB:

- Upholds the highest standards of excellence and integrity;

- Provides quality service and promotes strong external partnerships;

- Develops a diverse, innovative, and well-trained work force in order to collectively achieve our goals; and

- Embraces learning and change in order to meet the challenges of the future.

TTB Stakeholders

TTB's stakeholders care about TTB's mission and how the Bureau performs.

Business	U.S. And State Governments & Associations	Citizens, Consumers, And Foreign Governments
ALCOHOL, TOBACCO, FIREARMS & AMMUNITION INDUSTRIES • Distilled Spirits Plants • Bonded Wine Premises • Breweries • Alcohol Importers & Wholesalers • Industrial Alcohol Producers & Users • Manufacturers and Users of Nonbeverage Alcohol Products • Tobacco Products Manufacturers • Tobacco Importers & Tobacco Export Warehouse Proprietors • Firearms and Ammunition Manufacturers **TRADE GROUPS** • Wine • Distilled Spirits • Beer • Tobacco • Alcohol Fuel Plants • Importers • Wholesalers	**FEDERAL AGENCIES** • Office of Management and Budget • General Accountability Office • Department of Agriculture • Department of Energy • Department of Homeland Security • Department of Justice • Federal Trade Commission • Food and Drug Administration • U.S. Fish and Wildlife Service • U.S. Trade Representative **DEPARTMENT OF TREASURY** • Bureau of the Public Debt • Departmental Offices • Internal Revenue Service **STATE AND LOCAL GOVERNMENTS AND RELATED ASSOCIATIONS** • National Association of State Attorneys General • Federation of Tax Administrators • National Conference of State Liquor Administrators • National Alcohol Beverage Control Association	**PUBLIC/ FOREIGN GOVERNMENTS** • U.S. • Europe • Canada • Mexico • South America • Australia • Asia • South Africa • New Zealand

Protect the Public

TTB enforces the laws and regulations that ensure regulated industry products are safe for consumption, people running TTB-regulated businesses are law-abiding citizens, and TTB-regulated businesses are legitimate. TTB licenses these industries, and our investigators travel throughout the country and its territories and commonwealths visiting distilleries, bonded wine premises, breweries, and tobacco products manufacturers to ensure that industry members are complying with TTB regulations. TTB assures that industry members use the right manufacturing practices and formulas, and that labels and advertisements are accurate. The investigators collect samples, and our laboratories analyze the products to make sure they are safe and accurately represented by the label.

TTB investigators conduct approximately 400 product integrity, trade practice, contamination, and consumer complaint investigations annually. For example, TTB detained mislabeled products, detected a tobacco product being imported as a mouth freshener, as well as discovered a company producing herbal fruit beverages that contained more than 0.5 percent alcohol thereby subjecting the product to tax, and a distilled spirits plant (DSP) using an herb with sedative properties in their product. These actions, among a great many others, demonstrate that TTB will continue to find more effective and efficient ways to protect the public.

Collect the Revenue

The United States levies and TTB collects excise taxes on the manufacture or sale, production of wine, distilled spirits, malt beverages, tobacco products, firearms and ammunition. In recent years, TTB has collected nearly $15 billion annually from the regulated industries that make these items. TTB

To meet its mission, TTB must maintain a staff of highly skilled and specialized employees. Our offices employ auditors; tax, labeling, and formulation specialists; investigators; and chemists to ensure that we can protect the public and collect the tax revenue from the regulated industries.

collected approximately 98 percent from the alcohol and tobacco industries. Alcohol and tobacco each represent about 49 percent of the annual tax receipts, and Firearms and Ammunition Excise Tax (FAET) represents approximately 2 percent. About 400 taxpayers account for roughly 98 percent of the annual excise tax collections.

As the third largest tax collection agency in the U.S. Government (after the Internal Revenue Service [IRS] and Customs and Border Protection [CBP]), TTB strives to improve service to the taxpayers and reduce their burden in complying with Federal laws. To help reach this goal, TTB moved from random selection of audit targets to risk-based selection. This move will help the organization achieve greater effectiveness and efficiencies in its field operations. Other areas where TTB is making strides to become more effective and efficient include:

- Working to increase compliance by using statistical methods to measure and analyze industry-wide compliance with tax laws;

- Performing personnel and financial background checks of all operating permit applicants as needed;

- Enhancing the amount and presentation of online information for taxpayers and other industry members to make complying with regulations easier;

- Providing regulations, forms, and other information in plain language format; and

- Continuing to create alternative excise tax return filing methods through e-Government solutions.

Management and Organizational Excellence

Organizational Structure. TTB is organized into headquarters operations and field-level operations. TTB maintains headquarters in Washington, D.C., laboratories in Beltsville, Maryland and Walnut Creek, California, National Revenue Center in Cincinnati, Ohio, the field audit offices and seven trade investigation offices strategically located in major cities throughout the United States and Puerto Rico. See Appendix I for a schematic breakout of TTB's organizational structure.

General Management. The Administrator heads TTB, a Bureau of the U.S. Department of the Treasury. The Administrator serves under the general direction of the Secretary of the Treasury and under the supervision of the Deputy Assistant Secretary, Tax, Trade, and Tariff Policy, Office of Tax Policy.

General management, under the leadership of the TTB Administrator and Deputy Administrator, is responsible for establishing policy and assuring that the administration of activities at TTB are in compliance with the policies and delegations of authority of the Secretary of the Treasury.

The Deputy Administrator oversees the Congressional Liaison, who serves as the point of contact on all congressional matters, and the Public Affairs Specialist, who is the Bureau's principal advisor on media affairs. The Deputy Administrator also supervises the Equal Employment Opportunity Officer at TTB, who ensures that every person has a right to work in an environment free from harassment and unlawful discrimination and has equal opportunities for jobs and advancement.

TTB general management also consists of the following offices:

1. **Assistant Administrator, Field Operations (FO).** FO provides assistance and advice to other Federal and State agencies, industry members, and the public to ensure effective tax and trade compliance with the Federal Alcohol Administration (FAA) Act, the Internal Revenue Code (IRC), the Alcoholic Beverage Labeling Act, and the Webb-Kenyon Act. FO also develops and implements programs and conducts tax audits and investigations of industry members or applicants seeking permits to enter into a TTB-regulated business.

2. **Assistant Administrator, Headquarters Operations (HQ Ops).** HQ Ops determines and publishes policy decisions regarding the regulation of the alcohol, tobacco, firearms, and ammunition industries and provides assistance and advice to industry members, other Federal and State agencies, foreign governments, and the public.

3. **Assistant Administrator, Management/Chief Financial Officer (MGT).** MGT provides human resources, facilities, procurement, training, and financial information and guidance to its customers.

4. **Assistant Administrator, Information Resources/Chief Information Officer (CIO).** The Office of the CIO provides effective and secure information technology (IT) solutions that allow TTB to carry out its mission without imposing undue burdens on industries that the Bureau regulates.

5. **Director, Equal Employment Opportunity / Diversity Advancement (EEO/DA).** The EEO/DA office provides leadership, direction, and guidance in carrying out TTB's commitment to equal employment opportunity and diversity by: developing, directing, and administering EEO policies; supervising the EEO activities; processing and managing all EEO discrimination complaints; and recommending actions for complaints filed.

6. **Chief Counsel (CC).** The CC provides legal advice to the Administrator, Deputy Administrator, and other officials within TTB, and is responsible for performing all the legal services connected to the laws under the jurisdiction of TTB.

7. **Director, Office of Inspection (INS).** The INS provides coordination and management of Bureau-wide and organizational segment reviews and internal investigations of TTB offices and programs.

8. **Executive Liaison for Industry and State Matters (ELIS).** ELIS develops and implements programs designed to provide harmonious relationships and effective interchanges between TTB, regulated industry members, and State alcohol regulatory and taxation agencies.

TTB Strategic Goals and Objectives

TTB's strategic goals and objectives help meet the mission and goals of the Department of the Treasury.

Treasury and TTB Strategic Plans Relationship		
TREASURY STRATEGIC GOALS AND OBJECTIVES	**TTB PROTECT THE PUBLIC (PTP) MISSION AND STRATEGIC GOALS**	**TTB OBJECTIVES**
Treasury Strategic Goal (Economy): U.S. and World Economies Perform at Full Economic Potential		
TREASURY ECONOMIC STRATEGIC OBJECTIVE: Improved economic opportunity, mobility and security with robust, real, sustainable economic growth at home and abroad. **Outcome:** Strong U.S. economic competitiveness.	**TTB PTP STRATEGIC GOALS** 1. **BUSINESS INTEGRITY:** Assure that only persons who carry permits as authorized by statute operate within the industries TTB regulates. 2. **PRODUCT INTEGRITY:** Help industry members comply with all Federal labeling and advertising requirements for their products. 3. **MARKET INTEGRITY:** Assure the alcohol marketplace is free from anti- competitive practices. 4. **EFFECTIVE AND EFFICIENT SYSTEMS TO PROMOTE ECONOMIC OPPORTUNITY:** Facilitate economic opportunity and growth by maximizing TTB PTP systems' effectiveness and efficiencies.	**TTB PTP OBJECTIVES** **TTB PTP 1.1.** Issue permits to qualified applicants. **TTB PTP 1.2.** Assure that no current industry members are linked to criminal or terrorist organizations, or are otherwise a prohibited person. **TTB PTP 2.1.** Assure that industry members provide full and accurate product information to the consumer. **TTB PTP 2.2.** Assure that industry members avoid prohibited language and misleading statements on their labels and advertising. **TTB PTP 3.1.** Identify and address unfair trade practices and barriers in the U.S. alcohol marketplace. **TTB PTP 3.2.** Identify and address barriers in the international marketplace. **TTB PTP 4.1.** Increase effectiveness and efficiencies of TTB Protect the Public processes and systems.

Treasury Strategic Goal (Security): Strengthened International Financial System Security and Enhanced U.S. National Security		
TREASURY SECURITY STRATEGIC OBJECTIVE:	**TTB PTP STRATEGIC GOAL**	**TTB PTP OBJECTIVES**
Minimized and neutralized threats to U.S. national security and international financial systems.	1. **BUSINESS INTEGRITY (Security):** Assure that only persons who carry permits as authorized by statute operate within the industries TTB regulates.	**TTB PTP 1.1.** Issue permits to qualified applicants. **TTB PTP 1.2.** Assure that no current industry member is linked to criminal or terrorist organizations, or is otherwise a prohibited person.

Treasury Strategic Goal (Finance): Effectively Managed U.S. Government Finances		
TREASURY STRATEGIC GOALS AND OBJECTIVES	**TTB COLLECT THE REVENUE (CTR) MISSION AND STRATEGIC GOALS**	**TTB OBJECTIVES**
TREASURY FINANCIAL STRATEGIC OBJECTIVE: Available cash resources to operate the government as needed without excess. **Outcome:** Revenue collected when due through a fair and uniform application of the law.	**TTB CTR STRATEGIC GOALS** 1. **VOLUNTARY COMPLIANCE:** Provide high quality service, while imposing the least regulatory burden. 2. **TAX VERIFICATION AND VALIDATION:** Promote voluntary compliance and eliminate or prevent tax evasion and other criminal conduct. 3. **EFFECTIVE AND EFFICIENT TAX COLLECTION:** Provide the most effective and efficient system for the collection of all revenue that is rightfully due.	**TTB CTR OBJECTIVES** **TTB CTR 1.1.** Improve service to the taxpayer and reduce the burden of compliance with Federal law [Service and Outreach]. **TTB CTR 2.1.** Promote voluntary compliance and prevent tax evasion and identify other criminal conduct in the regulated industries [Enforcement]. **TTB CTR 3.1.** Maximize electronic solutions [e-Gov].

TREASURY STRATEGIC GOALS AND OBJECTIVES	TTB MISSION SUPPORT STRATEGIC GOAL AND OBJECTIVE	TTB OBJECTIVES
TREASURY MOE STRATEGIC OBJECTIVE: Constructive contribution to Americans' quality of life through an enabled and effective Treasury Department. **Outcome:** A citizen-centered, results-oriented and strategically aligned organization. Exceptional accountability and transparency.	**TTB MOE STRATEGIC GOAL** 1. **MANAGEMENT-SUPPORTED OPTIMUM PROGRAM EFFECTIVENESS AND EFFICIENCY:** Ensure that all TTB programs operate at optimum efficiency and effectiveness and with full accountability, by providing high quality management and administrative support.	**TTB MOE OBJECTIVES** **TTB MOE 1.1.** Implement a performance-based management system for meeting TTB's mission. **TTB MOE 1.2.** Deliver streamlined, flexible, and robust IT solutions that maximize the performance, value, and results to enable TTB to fulfill its mission and goals. **TTB MOE 1.3.** Use financial management systems to support TTB strategic management and financial accountability by providing information that is useful, timely, and reliable, and that assists TTB in optimizing decision-making. **TTB MOE 1.4.** Manage human capital to support TTB programs and the achievement of Bureau goals by building and sustaining a work environment conducive to performance excellence and personal and organizational development.

Executing the Strategic Plan

TTB subscribes to the Department of the Treasury's Integrated Management System. To accomplish its strategic objectives effectively, the Department of the Treasury and TTB must link outcomes, strategy, budget, and the production of value into an integrated management system. This management system, based on a model of continuous improvement, is shown below.

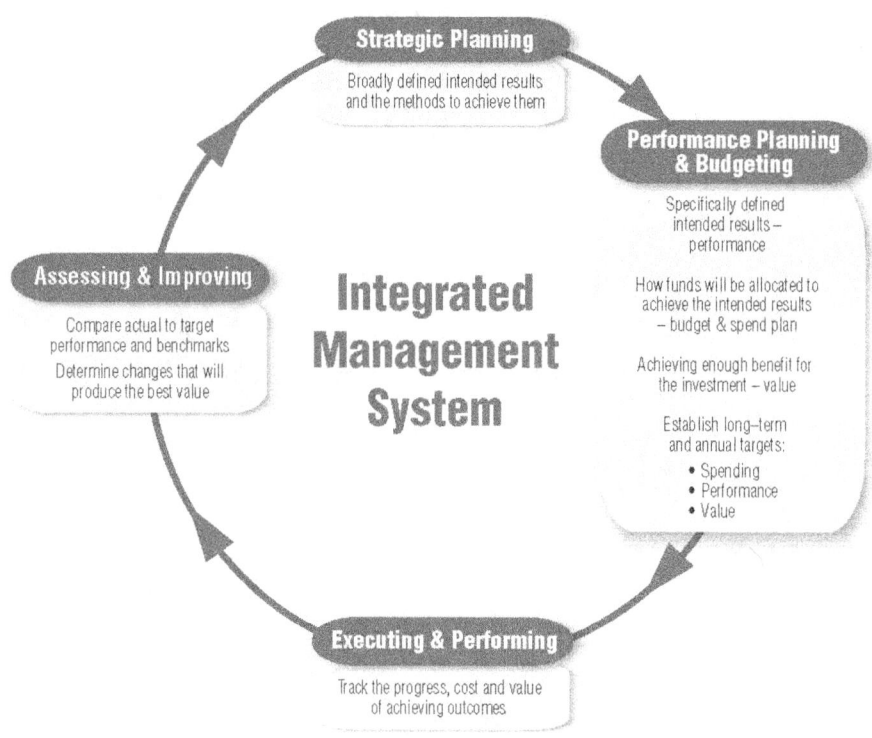

Protect the Public Mission

Business Integrity Strategies

Treasury Strategic Goals
Economy: U.S. and World Economies Perform at Full Economic Potential **Security:** Prevented Terrorism and Promoted the Nation's Security Through Strengthened International Financial Systems

The National Revenue Center (NRC) and the Trade Investigations Division (TID) work together to increase the effectiveness and efficiency of the NRC's telephonic permit process to ensure that only people with permits or qualification operate in the industries TTB regulates and to establish better telephonic methodologies based on lessons learned as a result of field investigations. Reciprocity with State authorities will also provide better resource utilization as well as establish mutual lessons learned between State and TTB authorities.

Using watchlists created by the Department of Homeland Security (DHS) or the Federal Bureau of Investigation (FBI) as well as scanning the International Trade Database System (ITDS) regularly will provide tools for increasing potential terrorism awareness for TTB's Trade Analysis and Enforcement Division (TAED) and the TID investigators. TTB will use these tools and others to expand the categories of prohibited persons.

Product Integrity Strategies

Treasury Strategic Goal
Economy: U.S. and World Economies Perform at Full Economic Potential

TTB's Advertising Labeling and Formulation Division (ALFD) will establish and pursue a market-based labeling and advertising compliance verification program. In the past, ALFD performed much of its work through certifying labels with limited understanding if the label that had been certified was actually the label that was on the product in the marketplace.

ALFD is currently undertaking a pilot study to pull product in the marketplace to test for regulatory compliance. ALFD will also seek to establish a statistically valid sample based on the results of a statistical study performed in FY 2007.

ALFD will also seek to increase compliance by initiating educational outreach programs through TTB's Web site, seminars, workshops, and Webcasts.

Treasury Strategic Goal
Economy: U.S. and World Economies Perform at Full Economic Potential

Several TTB divisions provide Federal Alcohol Administration Act seminars to educate industry members. The philosophy behind this approach is that industry members may comply through education or enforcement. Education may provide preventive or corrective action in helping industry members to comply. A seminar provided on industry member Web sites is one example of a tool that TTB may use to reach the maximum number of industry members through cooperative partnerships. Also, TTB needs to ensure that its employees are well-trained to help provide industry members the information they need to comply. Training employees in-house through on-the-job training will provide brush-ups and internal techniques that will increase knowledge transfer and sharing.

Where education falls short or through purposeful intent an industry member fails to comply, TTB will send letters to industry members, for example, in cases of prohibited inducements. The first or second letter may allow industry members to explain their actions. A successive letter may result in an investigation.

To expand the scope of operation, TTB investigators and other TTB divisions will work with State Alcohol Beverage Control Boards. Information sharing will likely be beneficial to all organizations concerned. Polling wholesalers will lead to further understanding of acceptable behavior in regulatory compliance.

Establishing successful trade practice cases will help TTB to enhance industry compliance. By publicizing successful cases, TTB can reinforce the importance of compliance. The establishment of a market-based labeling and advertising compliance verification program will further assure that the market is free from anti-competitive practices by increasing field time in the review of labeling and advertising.

Working to comply with an importing country's laws and regulations is important to U.S. industry members. This will require greater cooperation with foreign governments. As a consultant group, TTB's International Trade Division (ITD) must continue to educate the U.S. Trade Representative (USTR) concerning what is important to TTB's regulated industry members. It is important for ITD to note, in conjunction with the USTR, the limitations and barriers to doing business in other countries. This effort will likely result in developing memoranda of understanding with foreign countries, which will encourage working relationships between TTB and its foreign counterparts and provide TTB with a stakeholder's role.

Effective and Efficient Systems Strategies

Economy: U.S. and World Economies Perform at Full Economic Potential

TTB Protect the Public objectives require in-depth analysis to assure that TTB is facilitating economic opportunities effectively and efficiently. These objectives and measures are meant to help establish the "bang for the buck" that the public receives for its tax dollars. The first step is to assure that TTB has a cost accounting system in place to ensure a reasonable estimate of the unit cost of various programs or sub-programs that will provide both managerial cost accounting data while reconciling to external cost accounting data (e.g., net cost statement).

The benefit to the public can only be measured by internal comparisons over time since TTB's programs are unique (e.g., no other Federal Government program offers a benchmark or benchmarks for comparison). TTB must diligently measure trends in unit costs to help establish the effectiveness and efficiencies of individual programs.

Collect the Revenue Mission

Outreach/Promote Cooperation

Treasury Strategic Goal
Finance: Effectively Managed U.S. Government Finances

The Bureau operates under the assumption that most industry members want to comply with the laws and regulations that govern the industry. However, statutory and regulatory complexity decreases the chances of voluntary compliance, as reported by the American Institute for Certified Professional Accountants in a recent Congressional hearing.

TTB dedicates a significant portion of its Collect the Revenue resources to outreach programs that educate industry members and, where possible, simplify the reporting and tax filing process. Through various workshops, seminars, and conferences, TTB provides plain language instructions and one-on-one attention to promote voluntary compliance and enhance cooperation and communication between TTB and its regulated industry members.

Enforcement Strategies

Treasury Strategic Goal
Finance: Effectively Managed U.S. Government Finances

While the majority of industry members comply voluntarily, TTB strives to ensure that the industry members comply with all TTB laws and regulations. Industry members who violate these laws and regulations take unfair advantage of those who comply thus creating a tax gap. It is imperative, therefore, that where outreach and cooperation fail to promote voluntary compliance, TTB take enforcement actions to eliminate or prevent tax evasion and other criminal conduct where it occurs.

Effective and Efficient Tax Collection Systems

Finance: Effectively Managed U.S. Government Finances

The Bureau has developed effective and efficient tax collection systems that:

1. Simplify the filing and reporting system;

2. Increase the probability of voluntary compliance; and

3. Provide one of the best ratios of administrative costs to collect taxes to the revenue collected in the Federal Government.

Furthermore, TTB supported legislation that reduces the number of filings that small businesses must provide in a given year. The legislation (Public Law 109-59 effective January 1, 2006) reduced costs to the small taxpayer as well as decreased the cost of collection for TTB.

Management and Organizational Excellence Mission

Treasury Strategic Goal
Management: Management and Organizational Excellence

Top management at TTB is accountable for general management responsibilities including leadership, performance culture, and job satisfaction, and other categories listed under Office of Personnel Management's Federal Human Capital Survey (FHCS). While TTB has scored above average in all categories on the survey, discussions with the Treasury Strategic Planning group and TTB's Strategic Planning workgroup assessed that, for purposes of this strategic plan, for the next five years TTB should concentrate on areas where it was least successful in the FHCS.

Human Capital

TTB's organizational experience is vast. We dedicate a significant portion of the Master Plan to human resources strategic planning. Of TTB's 529 employees, 330 (62.4 percent) are employed within the following position titles. The breakdown of these 330 employees is shown below.

Occupation Title	Total Within the Occupation	As % of Total TTB Population
Auditor	80	15.1
Attorney	17	3.2
Chemist	23	4.4
Investigator	75	14.2
Alcohol and Tobacco Specialist/Tax Specialist / Tax and Trade Specialist	135	25.5
Total	**330**	**62.4**

Employees Eligible to Retire.

The breakdown of the 133 employees eligible for retirement during the next five years is as follows:

Occupational Title	# Eligible to Retire	As % of Total of All Employees within the Identified Occupational Titles	As % of All Employees in the same Occupational Title	GS-9	GS-11	GS-12	GS-13	GS-14	GS-15	SES
Auditor	27	20.3	33.8	2		8		17		
Attorney	5	3.8	29.4						4	1
Chemist	3	2.3	13.0					2	1	
Investigator	31	23.3	41.3				27	4		
AT Spec/Tax Spec/Tax and Trade Spec	67	50	49.6		34	11	7	14	1	
Total	**133**			**2**	**34**	**19**	**34**	**37**	**6**	**1**

In light of the proportions of the original group of 330 employees, it is not surprising that the majority of those eligible for retirement are either Investigators or Alcohol and Tobacco Specialists, or Tax Specialists, or Tax and Trade Specialists. Of those immediately eligible for retirement, 73.7 percent (98 of 133) currently occupy positions with these titles. Especially notable is that 58.7 percent (78 of 133) of those currently eligible to retire are employed at the GS-13 level or above.

Information Technology

TTB's IT Strategic Framework aligns IT goals, priorities, and initiatives to the Administrator's priorities, goals, and objectives. This framework seeks to drive IT results by creating an integration strategy with the program offices. This alignment also ensures the development of IT performance measures, which drive behaviors required to achieve TTB's IT mission and vision.

TTB IT Strategic Framework

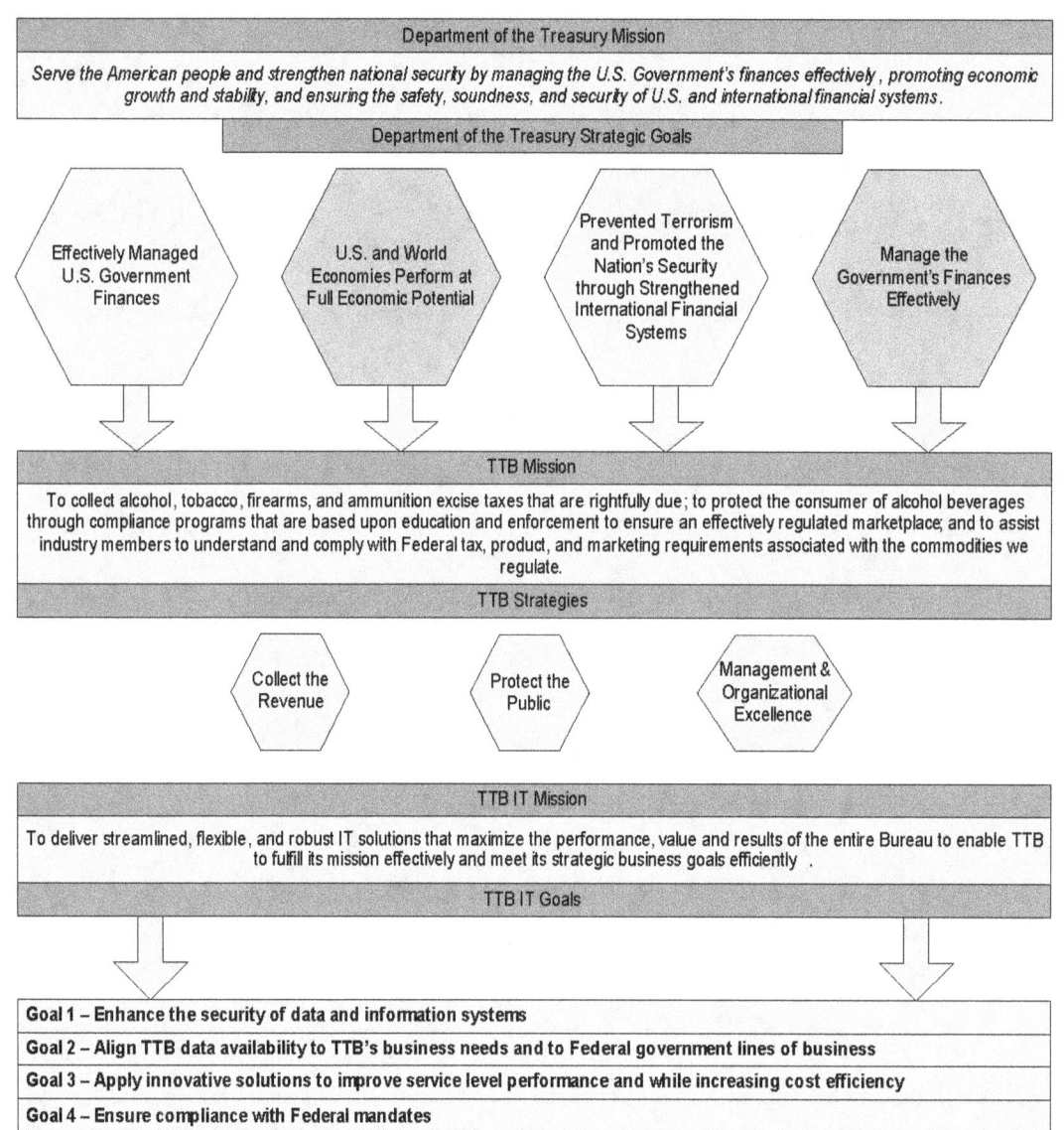

Department of the Treasury Mission

Serve the American people and strengthen national security by managing the U.S. Government's finances effectively, promoting economic growth and stability, and ensuring the safety, soundness, and security of U.S. and international financial systems.

Department of the Treasury Strategic Goals

Effectively Managed U.S. Government Finances

U.S. and World Economies Perform at Full Economic Potential

Prevented Terrorism and Promoted the Nation's Security through Strengthened International Financial Systems

Manage the Government's Finances Effectively

TTB Mission

To collect alcohol, tobacco, firearms, and ammunition excise taxes that are rightfully due; to protect the consumer of alcohol beverages through compliance programs that are based upon education and enforcement to ensure an effectively regulated marketplace; and to assist industry members to understand and comply with Federal tax, product, and marketing requirements associated with the commodities we regulate.

TTB Strategies

Collect the Revenue

Protect the Public

Management & Organizational Excellence

TTB IT Mission

To deliver streamlined, flexible, and robust IT solutions that maximize the performance, value and results of the entire Bureau to enable TTB to fulfill its mission effectively and meet its strategic business goals efficiently.

TTB IT Goals

| Goal 1 – Enhance the security of data and information systems |
| Goal 2 – Align TTB data availability to TTB's business needs and to Federal government lines of business |
| Goal 3 – Apply innovative solutions to improve service level performance and while increasing cost efficiency |
| Goal 4 – Ensure compliance with Federal mandates |

The IT Strategic Framework shows the clear linkage from business priorities identified by the Department of the Treasury to TTB IT goals. It also links TTB's strategic business needs with its capabilities to achieve the objectives of IT standardization, interoperability, compatibility, and fiscal discipline. The CIO is capturing this traceability and linkage by realigning TTB's IT systems to reflect industry standards and best business practices, while ensuring compliance with Federal mandates (e.g., Homeland Security Presidential Directive – 12, Record Management Initiative 5015.2, OMB Memoranda 05-22 and 07-16, Transition Planning for Internet Protocol Version 6 and Safeguarding Against and Responding to the Breach of Personally Identifiable Information, respectively) for application within the Federal Government. The CIO's priority is to maintain a well-led, high-performing IT organization that delivers responsive IT support to TTB program offices.

Strategic Alignment of Account Code Structure. Traditionally, budgets are not usually constructed around the organization's goals, but rather linked with organizations and programs, which makes it difficult to mesh budget and performance. At TTB we have solved this problem by introducing a new account code structure that we will apply during the FY 2008-2012 accounting periods.

This account code format will allow for the tracking of costs consistently from one year to the next, and capture critical strategic links in programs, goals, and major lines of business. The new coding will be used in both the core accounting system, and its various modules, and serves as an accounting and budget tool to help capture the strategic relationships between our inputs, the programs and activities that use those inputs, and the costs of the outputs that we create through the programs and activities.

The cost information that will be gathered from this process will help us better explain the value and relevant cost of our missions, goals, and programs to those outside of our organization, and improve our management over programs, as well as aid in the planning and decision-making process. Also, the application of the new "reporting category code" will capture valuable cost information that can be used in connection with process improvement efforts in our organization and serve as an integral part of our strategic planning process. The information known as "reporting category codes" will be captured along with other traditional budget categories such as cost center, object class, fund, budget fiscal year, and project codes.

Administrative Support Operations

Support Systems Integration. Many of TTB's administrative support systems such as travel, timekeeping, payroll, procurement, purchase cards, and human resources are integrated into the Oracle Federal Financial system (core accounting), and capture information and business transactions. The diagram below displays the high degree of complexity and array of systems that impact the core accounting system.

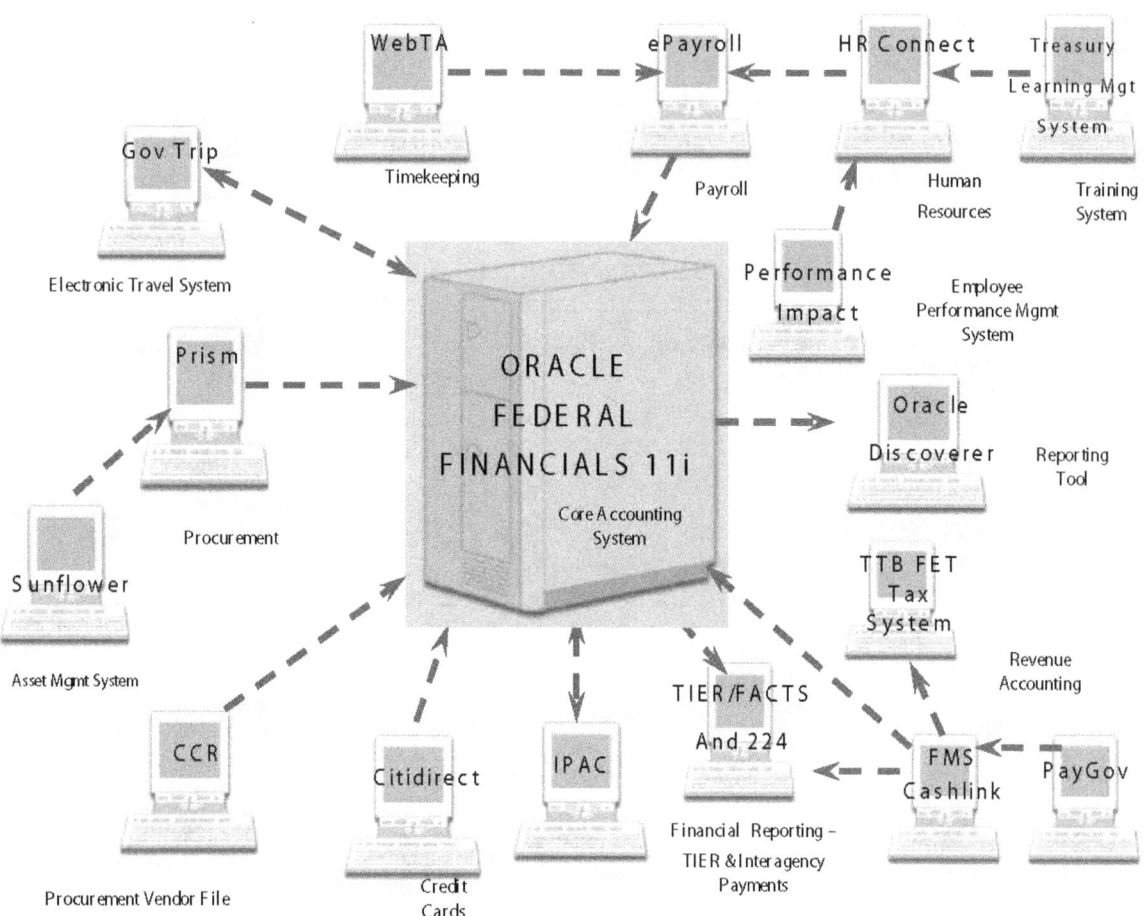

TTB also has several automated systems separate from the core accounting system. These systems are standalone, commercial off-the-shelf products and primarily serve as information repositories for asset management (Sunflower), employee performance (Performance Impact), and employee development (Treasury Learning Management System). Not all of these systems have automatic exchanges that feed into the core accounting system, but in many cases data is extracted from one system and entered into other systems.

Franchised Administrative Services. Initially, accomplishing the collect the revenue and protect the public mission objectives at TTB would have required building an administrative infrastructure comprised of financial and management systems, resources, and human capital. The fundamental cornerstone in setting up the administrative structure in support of these core business services was to ensure that the business strategy would support all TTB programs and enable them to operate at optimum efficiency and effectiveness. The long-term success of the Bureau depends on the administrative support to deliver the highest quality services in the areas of management and financial systems, while providing outstanding customer service to the TTB program staff.

However, TTB realized that to accomplish this objective, the organization needed to embrace a business strategy that placed a heavy reliance on outsourcing most of its administrative and information technology support services. When the Bureau was established, a skeleton number of staffing positions were authorized to provide the administrative support structure. By design, TTB was compelled to pursue an alternative service provider. As a result, in FY 2004, TTB began to separate its administrative support services from ATF, including its time and attendance, procurement, human resource, travel, property, and accounting and financial management services. TTB negotiated a reimbursable services agreement with the Bureau of Public Debt's Administrative Resource Center (BPD ARC), the key administrative services provider of Treasury's Franchise Fund.

The agreement included numerous performance standards for the service provider to achieve. Typifying public-to-public competitive outsourcing, this performance-based agreement between BPD ARC and TTB covers financial, payroll, human resources, procurement, asset management, and travel services.

After transitioning its human resource function over to BPD ARC, the next and most complex step was to transition the financial records, including its tax records from multiple accounting systems that had been used during the past decade. Beginning in FY 2005, TTB migrated its financial operations to BPD ARC, including key legacy tax information. This successful migration was fully completed during FY 2006, and included a multi-phase project that transferred the legacy tax data into the BPD ARC repository for tax information from multiple financial systems maintained at ATF and at U.S. Customs.

Strategy for Future Franchised Services. TTB anticipates a long-term partnership with BPD ARC. Highlights derived from this partnership include:

- Since 2004, BPD ARC has been providing the Bureau with administrative support in the areas of accounting, travel, payroll, human resources, and procurement with a focus on excellence and superior service.

- The human resource function is a full service arrangement and includes employee relations; staffing, recruitment, and classification; personnel actions and payroll processing; employee benefits and retirement; personnel security (now performed through the Department of the Treasury); time and attendance (through WebTA); and drug testing.

- The BPD ARC mission is to aid in improving overall Government effectiveness by delivering responsive and cost-effective administrative support to its customers, thereby improving the customers' ability to effectively discharge their mission.

- While the efficiency goals are somewhat reflective of the private sector, Federal regulations are perpetually evolving. This increasingly complex environment presents both challenges and opportunities in an administrative support services environment.

- The BPD ARC enterprise system eliminates the need for TTB to develop a unique set of accounting and management support systems. This Government enterprise solution provides the necessary budget and accounting system platform; provides key management reporting capability through Web-based pre-defined reports and an ad hoc reporting tool (e.g., Discoverer); and also provides a number of integrated systems to support our core business activities. As described previously, implementation of the WebTA timekeeping system, for instance, now allows TTB to track its direct labor costs and indirect costs for its core budget activities, strategic goals, programs, and specific projects.

In summary, this partnership allows TTB to focus staff resources and energies on core business applications.

In addition to the basic administrative services mentioned above covered under the BPD ARC agreement, TTB operates a Training and Professional Development Division (TPD) that is dedicated to enhancing the future of the agency by facilitating the professional development of all TTB personnel. The Treasury Learning Management System is used to facilitate training requests and procurement actions for those services.

APPENDIX A:
Environmental Scanning & Emerging Issues

Revenue from Excise Tax Collections

TTB will likely maintain its current revenue base for the foreseeable future (e.g., through 2010) based on the trends that have become evident over the past 10 years and projected into the future. While the past is not necessarily a predictor of the future, the past data has been moderately predictable for both tobacco and alcohol beverages. There is a slight bias toward slightly reduced revenues for alcohol and tobacco combined.

Tobacco Sales and Excise Tax Collections. Tobacco sales in the U.S. are expected to decrease slightly, based on our research. TTB expects a 4 to 5 percent decline from 2007 through 2012. This decline will be based mostly on a decline in cigarette sales. In 2006, cigarettes accounted for 76 percent of taxes collected and therefore, will likely determine future collections in the tobacco arena. From 2003 through 2006, there was a total decrease in cigarette collections of 5 percent. Although the Centers for Disease Control and Prevention reports that the smoking rate (number of smokers) has remained relatively unchanged over the past six years, TTB estimates that the amount these smokers consume has diminished. With the economy slowing, and the passage of cigarette tax increases by States and indoor smoking restrictions, this downward collections trend will likely continue.

Within some of the other areas of the tobacco industry, TTB expects large cigar sales to remain relatively unchanged or to dip slightly in a weakening economy. Large cigar sales accounted for 23 percent of tobacco collections in 2006. Small cigars, snuff,

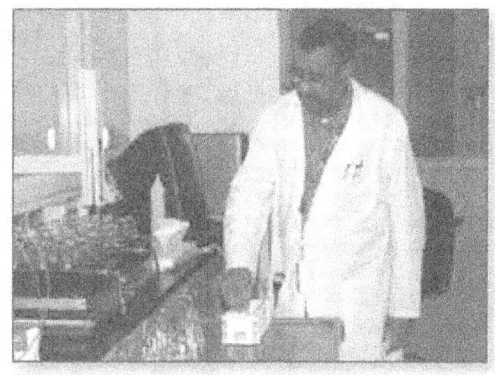

TTB Establishes Tobacco Laboratory

In FY 2008, the Scientific Services Division established the Tobacco Laboratory to refocus TTB efforts in the area of tobacco analyses. The new lab will enable expedited responses to the industry and growth in our technical ability.

The mission of the Tobacco Laboratory includes:

* Supporting tax classification for any tobacco product submitted by customers

* Supporting investigations of tobacco industry by TTB auditors and investigators

* Providing technical support to State tax authorities on tobacco products

* Providing technical support to other Federal agencies on tobacco-related issues

The Tobacco Laboratory will work with the laboratory staff of domestic and international tobacco regulatory agencies for the purpose of sharing and enhancing technical expertise on tobacco.

This shift in focus will give our staff the time needed to expand our expertise and our technical capabilities in analyzing tobacco.

chewing tobacco, pipe tobacco, and roll-your own tobacco combined accounted for approximately 1 percent of total tobacco collections, consistent with the previous 3 years, and will more than likely stay consistent over the next 5 years, with roll-your-own tobacco sales possibly becoming a more attractive alternate to traditional cigarettes or other types of tobacco. There could be modest increases in snuff and chewing tobacco sales as the big tobacco industries are becoming interested in producing and marketing these alternatives to cigarettes.

Another factor that could significantly affect future tobacco sales is the State Children's Health Insurance Program (SCHIP) or similar legislation that would increase the Federal excise tax on tobacco products. The bill is scheduled to be revisited in 2009. During a similar tax increase in 2000, tobacco taxes levels jumped 23 percent over the previous year. If the proposed SCHIP increase passes, TTB expects a similar increase in collections if history is any indicator.

Cigarette Consumption

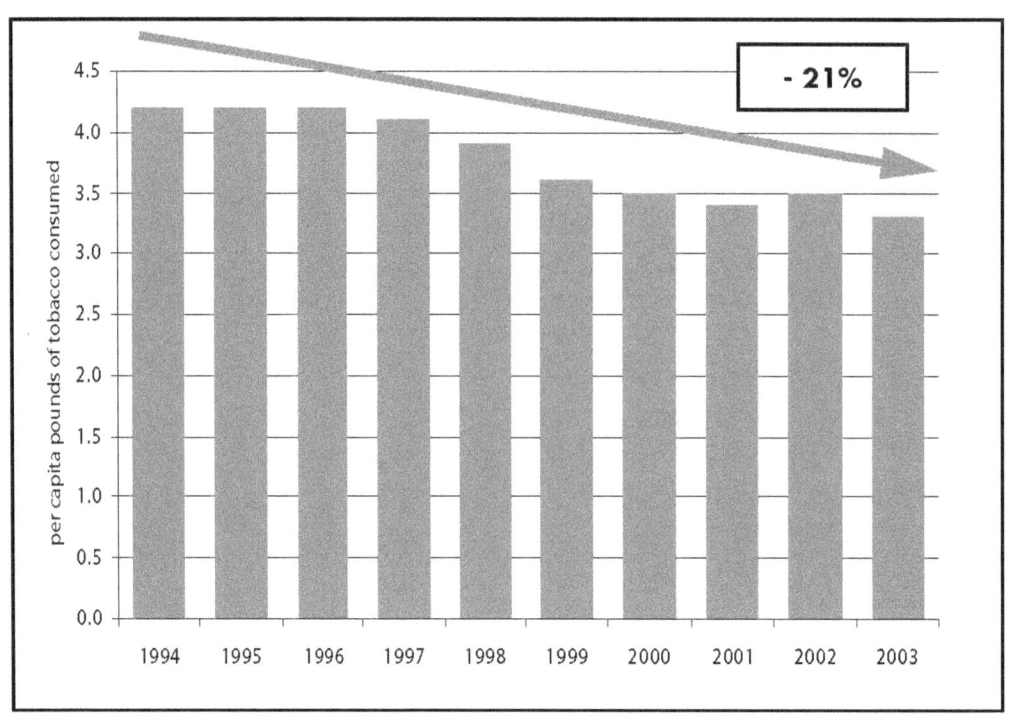

Source: USDA, Economic Research Service

Chewing Tobacco Consumption

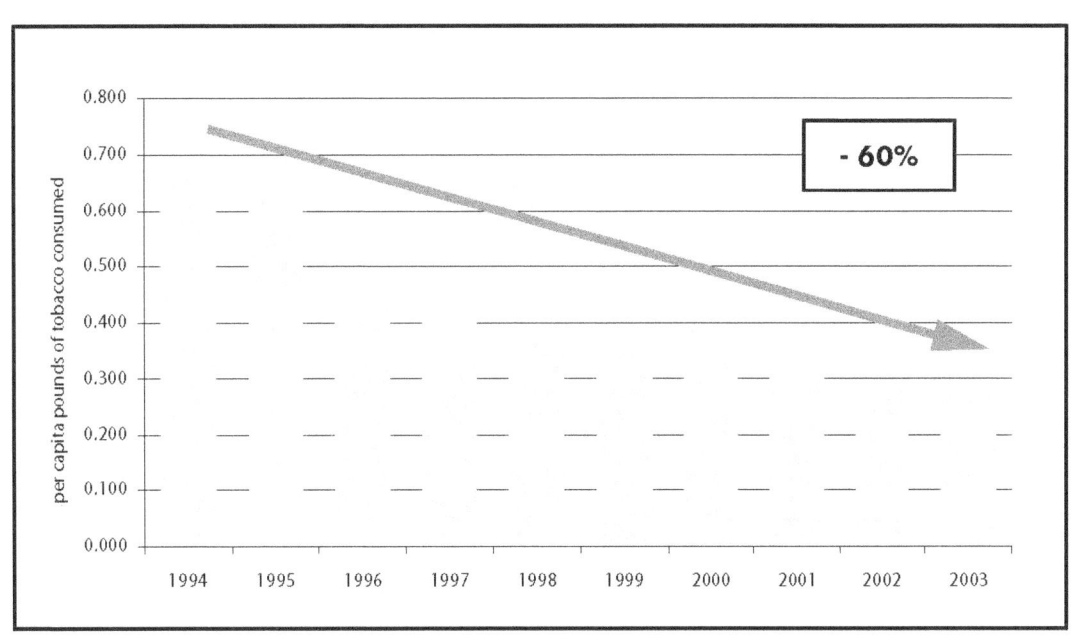

Source: USDA, Economic Research Service

U.S. Cigarette Consumption & Wholesale Price

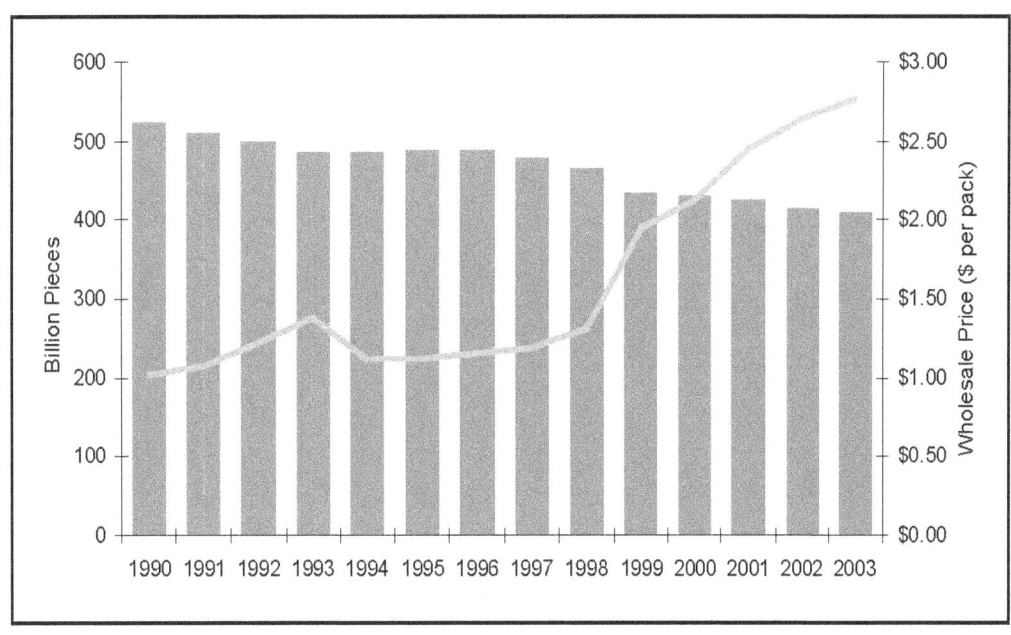

Source: USDA, Economic Research Service

Alcohol Beverages Consumption and Excise Tax Collections.

Alcohol beverage consumption had decreased marginally from 1990 through 1995. The trend, however, has been up since then although the percentage of increase appears to be decreasing. Substitutions should occur through 2015 as beer drinkers turn to wine and distilled spirits consumption. Two variables that influence wine consumption are age and income. With the onset of Baby Boomers, these variables favor more wine consumption and less beer drinking. Spirits should also increase significantly over time.

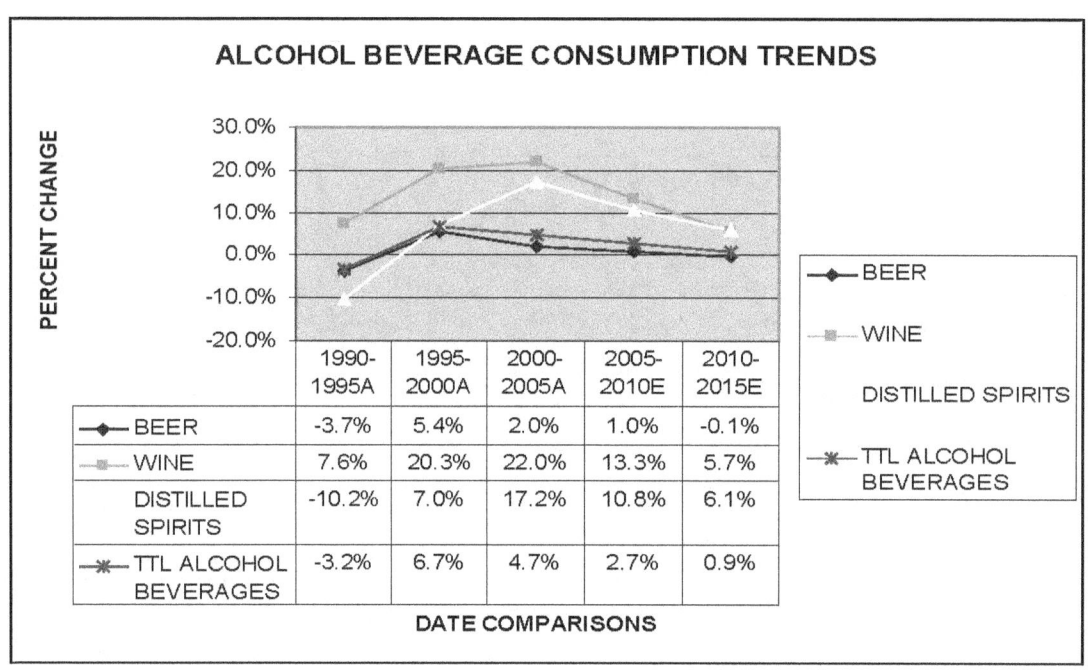

ALCOHOL BEVERAGE CONSUMPTION TRENDS

	1990-1995A	1995-2000A	2000-2005A	2005-2010E	2010-2015E
BEER	-3.7%	5.4%	2.0%	1.0%	-0.1%
WINE	7.6%	20.3%	22.0%	13.3%	5.7%
DISTILLED SPIRITS	-10.2%	7.0%	17.2%	10.8%	6.1%
TTL ALCOHOL BEVERAGES	-3.2%	6.7%	4.7%	2.7%	0.9%

At this point, the best estimate is a flat to slightly upward trend line for alcohol consumption when taking into account substitution of wine and distilled spirits drinking for beer drinking.

Beer Excise Tax Collections

The amount of beer tax that is collected by TTB is directly related to domestic consumption. The tax on imported beer is collected by CBP. In recent years, the amount of beer tax collected has ebbed and flowed but remained within a moderately tight range.

Going forward, beer will become more expensive to make and the consumer will likely see a price increase. Factors attributing to this include a more than 40 percent decline in the U.S. dollar (vs. Euro and UK Pound) over the past two years (e.g., ending in calendar year 2007), a 40 percent hike in the price of barley, a 32 percent hike in the price of hops, and a 28 percent increase in the price of glass for bottles.

So what impact will all of this have on consumption and by extension beer tax collection? Likely calendar year 2008 will end with beer tax collections falling within the historical range.

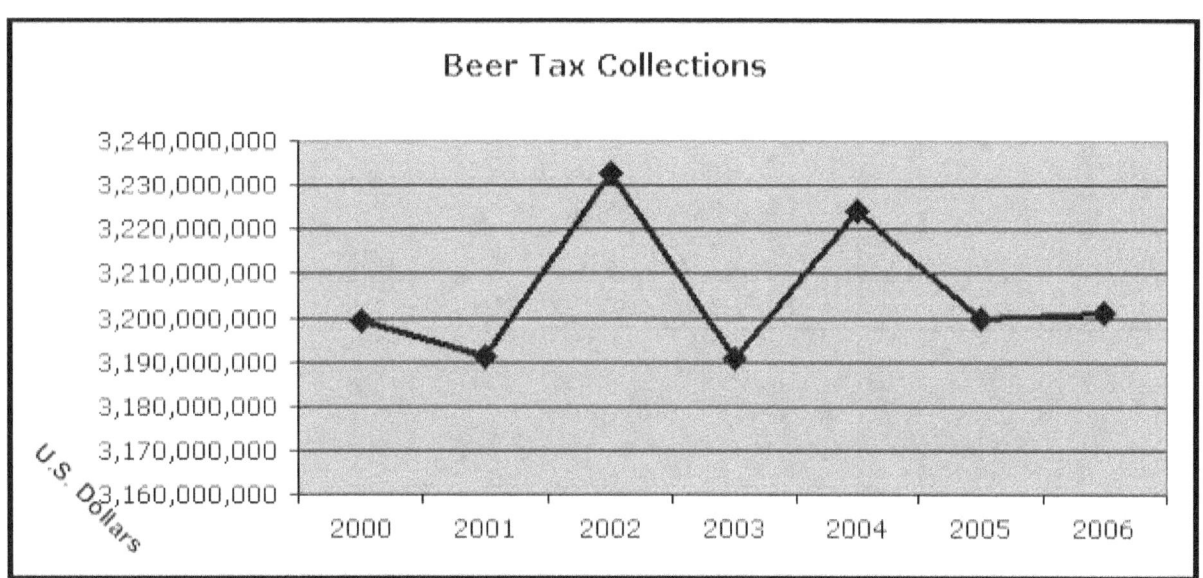

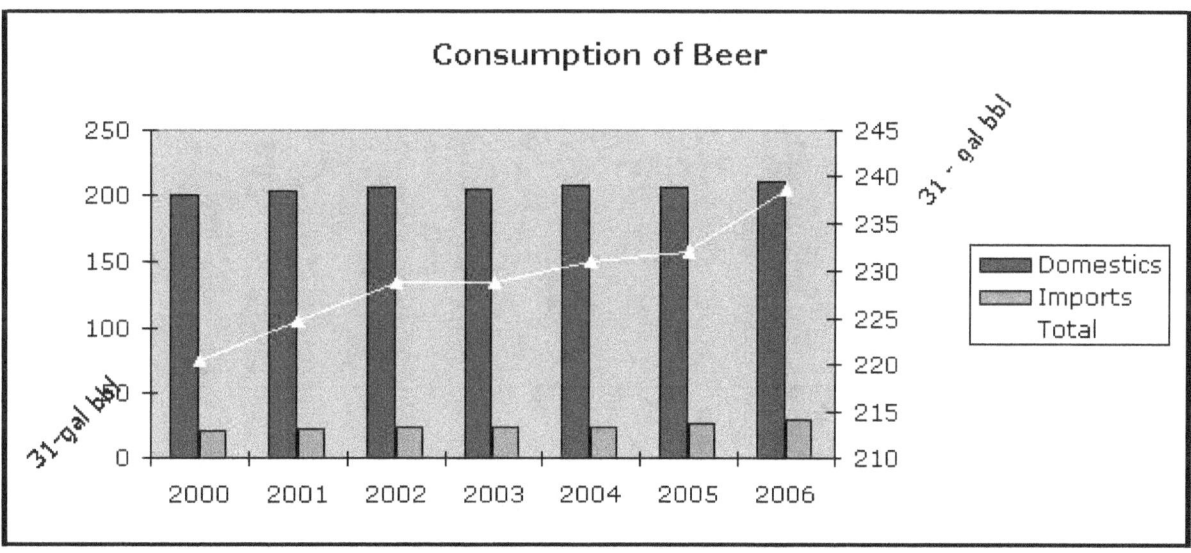

Forecasts for the beer industry in 2008 include:

- The current trend of trading up (from economy brands to premium brands) will slow down. One would think this would hurt crafts and imports; however, it could end up being a positive thing in that drinkers trade down from the higher priced wine and spirits to craft beer and imports. Economy brands will likely prosper.

- Craft beers have been hit by the high commodity costs and a slowing economy. Some questions for craft brewers going forward are, "Will the growing consumer trend of indulging in small luxuries continue?" and "If it does, is the brand equity and quality of craft beers strong enough to continue to grow the segment no matter what the economy dishes out?"

It would be difficult to predict beyond 2008 for beer tax collections. Based on past trends, the trend will likely be relatively flat and range bound.

Import of Malt Beverages
31 Gallon Barrels (1986 – 2006)

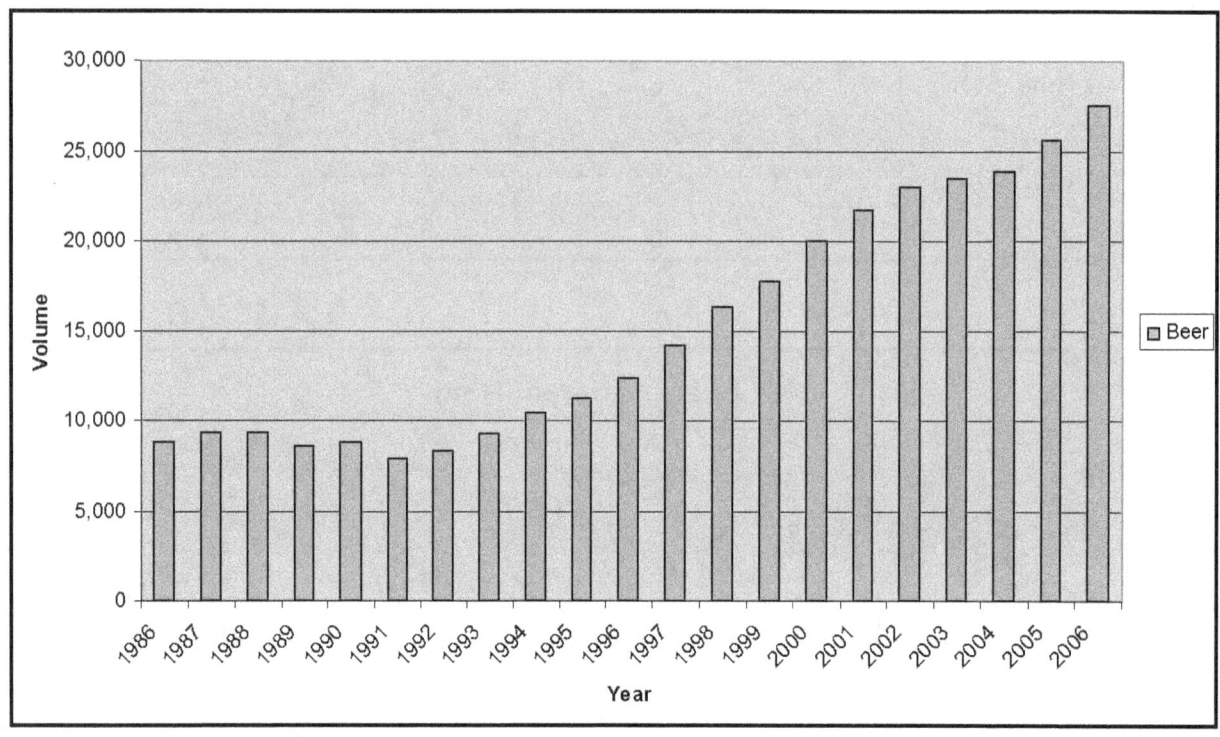

Domestic Malt Beverage Production
31 Gallon Barrels (1986 – 2006)

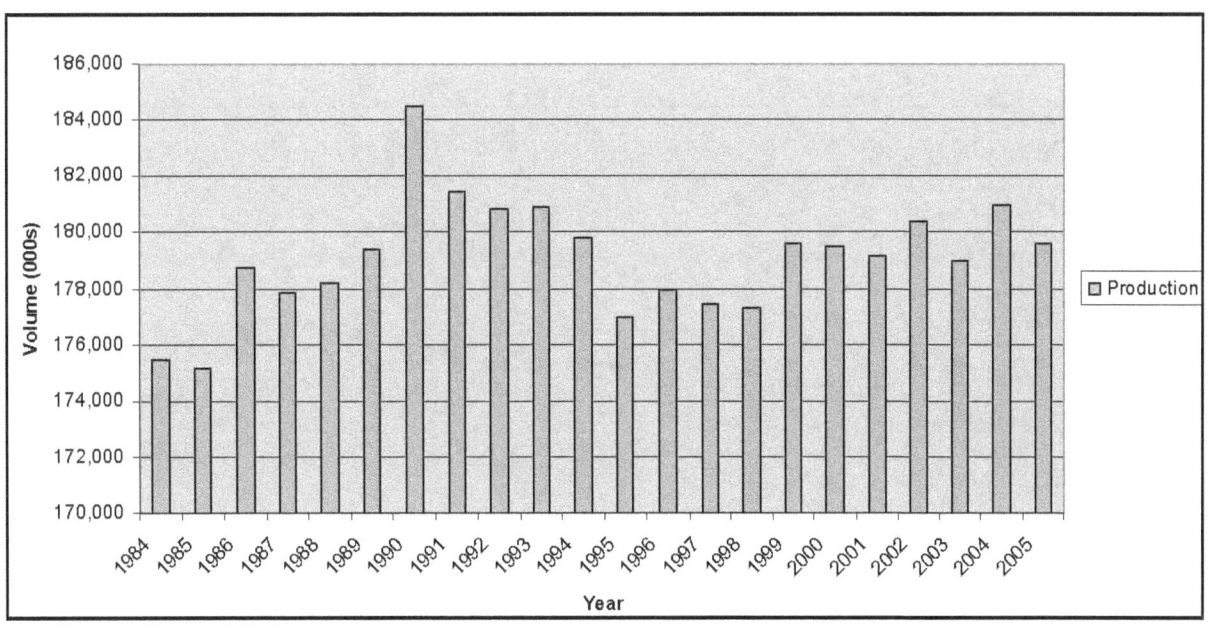

Distilled Spirits Excise Tax Collections

Based on historical trends, excise tax collections for distilled spirits are expected to increase as follows:

- The projection for vodka is for a 2 to 3 percent annual increase
- Projections for tequila are for a 3 percent increase,
- Rum is one-half of one percent, and
- Specialty products should increase approximately 2 percent.

Wine Excise Tax Collections

About 35 percent of U.S. adults drink wine. The rest of the adult population either does not drink any alcohol beverages, or prefer beer or distilled spirits. The per capita consumption of wine consumers in 2007 was estimated by the Wine Market Counsel to be 3.07 gallons (15 - 750 ml bottles, or 1.25 cases per year). Excise tax on domestic wine products accounts for less than 10 percent of the domestic alcohol tax collected by TTB.

The ratio of retail sales and consumption of domestic and imported wine in the early 1990s was typically 85 percent domestic and 15 percent imported wine. An increase in the importation of good quality, affordable wine from Italy, Australia, and South American countries has caused domestic wine sales to steadily lose ground to imported products.

The ratio in 2006 was 74 percent domestic wine to 26 percent imported wine, according to the Adams Wine Report. Analysts at the Unified Wine and Grape Symposium in January 2008 predicted that the imported wine share of the market may have been as high as 31 percent in 2007. It is expected that this trend will continue, as the volume of wine imported into the U.S. grows each year and the amount of wine produced domestically remains fairly steady.

Wine Excise Tax Collections

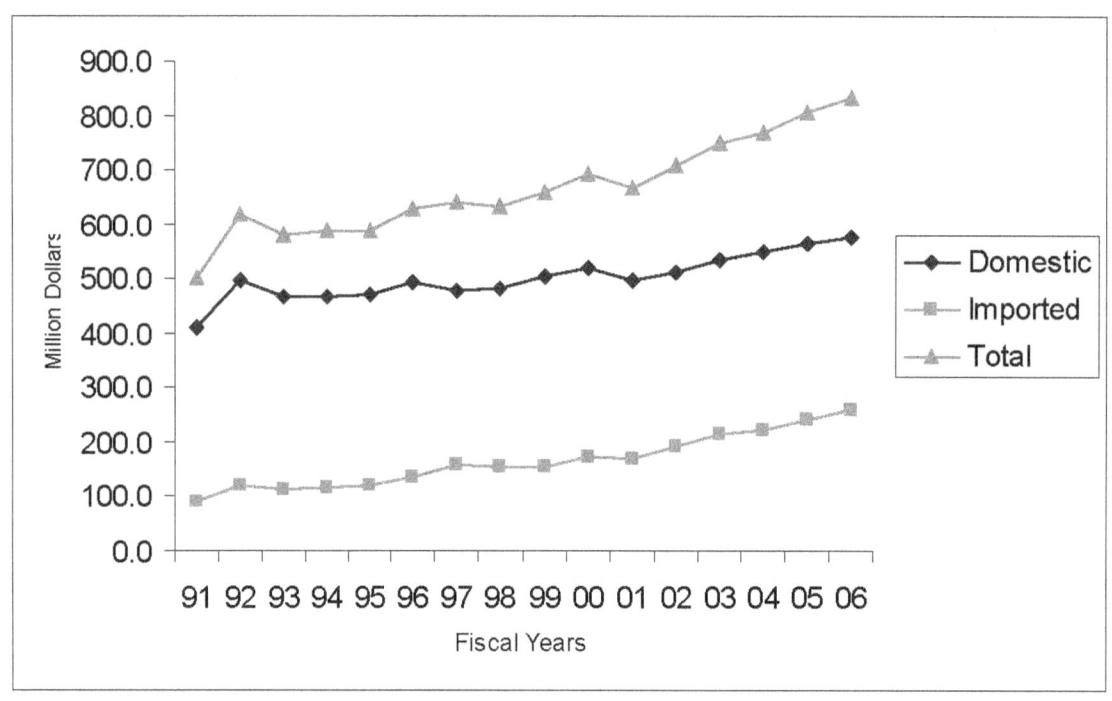

Bonded Wine Premises

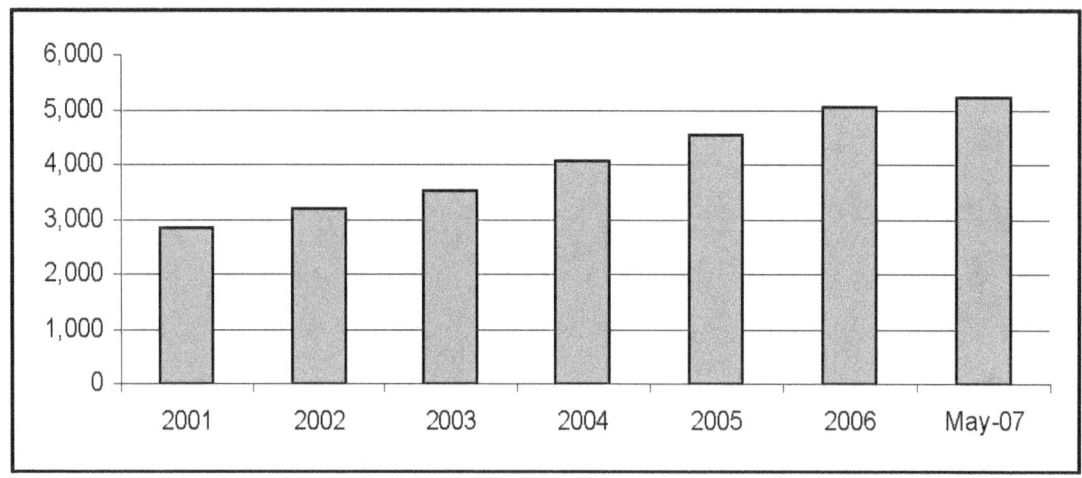

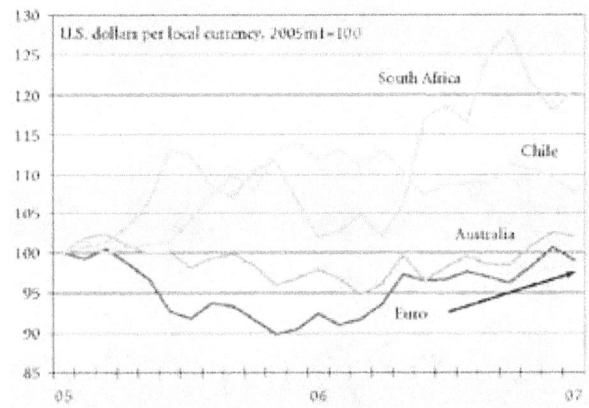

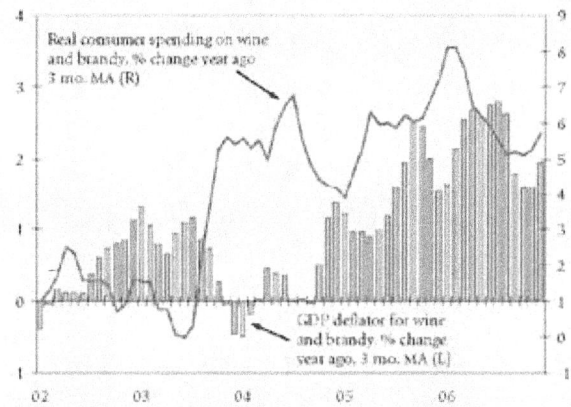

Moody's Industry.Com – Wine Industry

According to Moody's Industry.Com – Wine Industry (March 2007):

Fewer regulations are also helping vintners bolster bottom lines. Smaller wineries in particular have cashed in on the consumer trend of shifting to premium priced wine.

If the dollar continues to weaken further in coming years against most global currencies, this phenomenon will improve cost-competitiveness for domestic wine exports in key emerging markets in Asia, such as China, India, and Korea.

Long-Term Outlook: Improving name recognition and rising wine consumption globally are the positive fundamentals driving the industry's outlook. Wine is steadily gaining popularity among Americans, and currently rivals beer as their most preferred alcoholic drink.

The number of core wine drinkers—those who consume at least one glass of wine each week—has grown sharply since 2000 and now accounts for 17 percent of the total adult population and nearly 90 percent of wine consumption. Finally, the share of the core consumers in the population rises with age cohort, an encouraging sign in an aging country. At the same time, wine consumption is becoming increasingly popular with the millennial generation, which is nearly as large as their parent generation, the Baby Boomers. These two cohorts together already form a very large demand base of core wine drinkers and offer significant potential for growth.

Per capita consumption in the U.S. is still well below rates in Europe, suggesting potential for growth. As the Baby Boomer generation moves into its fifties and sixties, its disposable income will rise. There is a good likelihood that their demand for wine will rise as the economy improves, and their penchant for collecting luxury wines may increase as well.

Longer term, the wine industry will benefit from the new millennial generation of wine drinkers that will hopefully pick up the mantle as baby boomers age. The oldest of this new large cohort, almost as big as the baby-boomer cohort, are now in their early 20s, and 40 percent of this cohort are considered core wine drinkers. The challenge for the wine industry will be to deepen its attraction of marginal drinkers, who have cut their consumption of wine over the past three years.

The strategic threat of lower-cost wine with fruitier flavors from wineries in Australia, Chile, and South Africa is very real. Large wineries have reduced their exposure to this competition by acquiring properties in several of these areas, but local growers and small vintners will continue to be pressured by the cheaper and consumer-friendly wines from the New World wineries.

Upside Risks: The wine industry is making forays into several new markets, by re-branding. Success in these new strategies would also boost wine consumption. A further departure into higher priced wines by an adoring consumer base is also a possibility. Foreign markets also present some upside potential as untapped consumer markets in China, Russia, Southeast Asia, and the Middle East blossom.

Downside Risks: The most serious downside risk is from pestilence, specifically from the glassy-winged sharpshooter and its accompanying Pierce's disease, or from the vine mealy bug. There have been no significant pestilence problems reported thus far this season [2008], but this is a threat that bears watching.

Over the very long run, gradual global climate shifts could pose a serious threat to [various areas of the] wine industry. Temperature and precipitation patterns are already ideal and even subtle shifts could disrupt this delicate balance, with a potentially severe negative impact on the quantity and quality of wine produced in California.

The weakening of the U.S. dollar in 2006 against most major currencies gave some support to the wine industry. In particular, the dollar has weakened relative to most of the domestic wine industry's foreign competitors, except Chile. This allowed U.S. wine exports to rebound sharply in 2006, after falling in the previous year. The dollar is expected to continue depreciating against most currencies.

The domestic wine industry is still enjoying a boom period, thanks to steady growth in consumer demand for wine. Robust demand growth has come despite acceleration in prices for wine, which has been a double benefit to winemakers. With the housing market driving a broader economic slowdown, consumer spending is expected to moderate in the near future. This will weigh on demand growth during this period.

Permit Applications

The number of new, or original, permit applications is a good indication of future business. The following chart shows the growth in permits over recent years. New permit growth is offset somewhat by some industry members going out of business. This is particularly true as it pertains to the craft beer industry.

	Permit Applications – Original and Amended			
Fiscal Year	Original Permits	Amended Permits	Total	Percent Increase
2003	3,360	13,100	16,460	16%
2004	3,621	15,300	18,921	33%
2005	4,447	24,000	28,447	100%
2006	4,869	20,470	25,339	79%
2007	5,285	22,336	27,621	95%
2008 (P)	4,885	21,228	26,113	84%

APPENDIX B: Strengths, Weaknesses, Opportunities, and Threats (SWOT) Analysis

The Importance of Environmental Scanning

The previous sections provide a roadmap for aligning Treasury and TTB's missions, performance goals, and measures. The environmental scanning section provides an understanding for potential possibilities for organizational enhancement (Opportunities) and/or roadblocks (Threats) in achieving those goals. The SWOT Analysis was developed as a result of work in several areas: 1) the Environmental Scanning section; 2) the results of an Executive Management Meeting where workgroups of specialists/experts provided input/feedback for the SWOT Analysis; and 3) research performed by strategic planning personnel and interns; and 4) readily available studies and literature.

Strengths

- Continuance of interning, hiring, and training bright students and staff members for succession planning

- Pay banding helps to maintain mission-critical employees

- Strong IT department integrating new technological advancements as they evolve

- Good reputation among other bureaus and the public as a prospering new Treasury bureau

  - In an independent study in FY 2006, TTB was ranked as the tenth best place to work out of 222 programs

  - In the same study, TTB was ranked second as "family friendly" and sixth in its strategic management efforts

- Accessible knowledge/information within and outside of the organization's network

- Highly motivated and focused management and staff

- Fresh and innovative ideas for a newly founded Bureau

- Experienced and well-trained personnel

  - In-house and on-the-job training for the purpose of

    - Brush-ups

    - Internal techniques

- Small bureau enhances fast response times

- Regular staff meetings provide sound task distribution

- Network provides a free-flow of information to all personnel at their fingertips

- Managers and supervisors maintain an open-door, friendly environment for all employees

Weaknesses

- Many experienced and well-trained mission-critical personnel are eligible for retirement

  — Thirty percent of the Trade Investigations Division (TID) is currently eligible for retirement, including 57 percent of the District Directors and 100 percent of the Program Managers

  — Forty-three percent of TID is eligible for retirement within 3 years; 52 percent within 5 years

  — Full-time equivalent (FTE) resources in the future will include a need for the following areas where TTB is currently vulnerable:

    - Criminal investigators

    - Trade investigators

    - Regulations specialists

    - Lawyers, scientists, and other partners

- There have been significant increases in activities across the board at TTB since its inception; however, FTE levels have remained the same, which:

  — Puts stress on the system

  — Reduces in some instances TTB's ability to serve its customers with the same outstanding results that TTB achieved in the past

- Many CPA's and other professional job classifications are difficult to maintain because of extensive travel schedules, etc.

- Performing statistically-valid compliance requires a greater need for resources

  — More analytical resources

  — A significant paradigm shift that, if implemented, may take away resources from referrals of non-compliance or possible criminal activities

- As a small bureau, upward mobility among employees may be limited

- Non-defense or non-bioterrorism organizations are under budgetary pressures

- As a new bureau, IT platform requirements, etc. require funding that may not be available in the future

- Achieving needed regulatory and legislative requirements are often laborious, or non-existent

- Need attachés for specific country expertise (e.g., Brussels, China, etc.) and with international trade expertise

Opportunities

- TTB's reputation for its openness and honesty among Government and non-Government entities allows the organization to maintain strong networking that supports TTB's results-oriented persuasion

- TTB's experienced personnel may place it in a position of strength should further business (social benefit) opportunities arise

- Reciprocity with State authorities and interagency agreements allow TTB to leverage its resources

    — Law enforcement and regulatory organizations

    — State Alcohol Control Boards, etc.

- A strong IT group provides technical solutions to many of TTB's FTE resource limitations

    — Development of communication tools will provide TTB with effective and efficient means to collaborate internally and externally (e.g., SharePoint and GovDelivery)

- Pay.gov and other automated services provide opportunities to increase effectiveness and efficiencies for TTB and its customers

- Determination of customer expectations will help TTB to establish standards and periodically reassess customer needs and requirements

- Working toward fund sharing through the following programs will help offset TTB reliance on appropriations and will allow TTB to increase its presence in risk-induced areas:

    — Treasury Forfeiture Fund

    — Recovery cost of managing the FAET Program, which would require a statutory change

- Establishing and pursuing a market-based labeling and advertising compliance verification program will help TTB close the loop in determining if industry members are actually compliant in the marketplace

- TTB has an opportunity to increase voluntary compliance with results developed through education provided on TTB's Web site, seminars, workshops, and Webcasts

- The Federal Alcohol Administration (FAA) Act seminars help educate industry members

- Publicizing successful enforcement cases will provide impetus for other non-compliant industry members to re-evaluate unacceptable behavior

- Memoranda of Understanding (MOUs) with foreign countries to establish a point of contact on trade and regulatory issues

- Harmonize standards (e.g., U.S. biggest importers)

- Promote U.S. laws among international industries dealing with products regulated by TTB to ensure that the international industries understand and respect U.S. laws

- TTB needs to work with other countries to ensure cooperation as TTB attempts to work around the political realities of other countries

- TTB needs to consult with the U.S. Trade Representative in terms of what is important to the industry as well as publicizing what is required to do business in other countries.

- TTB needs to develop and implement a Criminal Enforcement Program

- TTB needs to establish a flexible organization that anticipates change and develops strategies to prepare for changes (e.g., tobacco, Alcohol Fuel Plants, excise taxes, etc.)

Threats

- Terrorism requires that TTB be vigilant in metropolitan, as well as rural (e.g., Alcohol Fuel Plant) settings with limited resources to cover geographically-expansive areas

- The lack of law enforcement agents reduces TTB's effectiveness in many areas

- Legal impediments slow down the process or keep TTB from performing some of its mission

- Policy decisions require TTB to work without critical analytical tools (e.g., fingerprinting capabilities)

- The identification of non-compliant advertising, especially as it relates to Internet advertising that is rising exponentially, is increasing in difficulty with limited resources

- The need for laboratory services is increasing while FTEs and funding remains nearly the same

    - The lab has $70,000 in funding for allergens in FY 2007 while the prospect for increased requirements is increasing significantly

    - Varietal identification requires more global definition

- As a new and small organization, TTB must ensure its survival by consistently establishing its ability to show its unique strengths to perform its mission

- TTB's loss of knowledge, with mission-critical personnel potentially retiring over the next several years, may weaken its impact within the industries and Government management without clear succession planning

- Continuous changes in business models will require constant vigilance

- The laws that help TTB regulate the industry are often difficult to prove

- Industry members are often unaware of regulatory requirements

- TTB regulations need updating to ensure that industry members understand the most recent implementations

TTB has established Memoranda of Understanding (MOUs) with other Federal agencies, including:

- **Bureau of Public Debt (BPD).** TTB reached an agreement to franchise out its financial systems requirements to the Bureau of Public Debt's Administrative Resource Center (BPD ARC), which uses an established Joint Financial Management Improvement Program (JFMIP) Oracle Financial System. In addition, TTB franchised most of our personnel, procurement, partial budget, and e-travel functions. This partnership has resulted in cost savings to TTB, while helping ARC meet its revenue goals and expected customer satisfaction requirements.

- **Food and Drug Administrations (FDA).** TTB examines alcohol beverage labels and routinely tests product samples for compliance with laws and regulations. When label/product analysis indicates a potential risk to public health or safety, immediate action is required. Any food product (including an alcohol beverage) is considered adulterated under the Federal Food, Drug, and Cosmetic Act if it contains a poisonous or deleterious substance or an unapproved food additive.

  Contaminated alcohol beverages will be considered adulterated for purposes of the Food, Drug, and Cosmetic Act and subject to enforcement action by the FDA, as determined by TTB. Under the terms of the MOU between the two agencies, TTB will notify the FDA when an adulterated alcohol beverage is encountered, request a health hazard assessment (as needed), seek a voluntary recall (as needed) and keep the FDA apprised of the situation.

- **U.S. Department of Agriculture (USDA).** On October 21, 2002, the USDA finalized rules implementing the National Organic Program. This Program establishes national standards for the production and handling of organically produced products, including alcohol beverages. Consequently, the USDA and TTB share in the regulatory control of alcohol products that bear an organic claim on their label. A recent MOU between the USDA and TTB establishes procedures that allow for a timely concurrent review of these labels to ensure that they comply with all Federal labeling regulations.

- **Bureau of Alcohol, Tobacco, Firearms, and Explosives (ATF).** TTB and ATF have signed an information-sharing MOU that gives both bureaus access to the information essential for the accomplishment of their programs. This includes investigations of diversion of alcohol and tobacco products to avoid tax payment.

  Bureau personnel also work with other Federal and State agencies in the regulation of the alcohol and tobacco industries. For example:

- **U.S. Immigration and Customs Enforcement (ICE).** The Homeland Security Act of 2002 created this agency and U. S. Customs and Border Protection (CBP) within the Department of Homeland Security to enforce U. S. customs laws. These agencies are now responsible for enforcement and collection of tobacco excise taxes when tobacco products are in CBP's custody. TTB is coordinating its IRC tobacco enforcement activities with ICE and CBP enforcement of the Cigarette Smuggling Act of 2000.

- **U. S. Customs and Border Protection (CBP).** TTB also interacts with CBP in the area of alcohol and tobacco importation. TTB often provides CBP with confirmation that TTB has issued a Certificate of Label Approval (COLA) for imported beverage alcohol products and that TTB has licensed individuals as alcohol or tobacco importers. TTB also verifies the authenticity or classification of alcohol beverage products to ensure that the proper excise tax and duty rates are applied.

  TTB often consults with CBP to determine information about the importer of record for various alcohol and tobacco products and to verify if certain products have been imported into the United States. TTB fills an important role, along with several other Federal agencies, in assisting CBP in the development of an integrated International Trade Data System (ITDS). This database provides a data tracking mechanism instrumental to meeting the requirements of the Bioterrorism Act of 2002, which requires that we verify the authenticity of commercial goods being shipped into U.S. ports.

- **Office of the U.S. Trade Representative (USTR).** In the area of U.S. trade policy, TTB works very closely with the USTR to create worldwide opportunities for economic development and technological progress. As part of a USTR interagency work group, TTB serves as technical advisor and authority on U.S. alcohol beverage laws, regulations, and policy. In this capacity, TTB provides assistance to the USTR in alcohol beverage and tobacco matters within the World Trade Organization Council on Trade-Related Aspects of Intellectual Property, its Technical Barriers to Trade Committee, and other groups. Through these activities, TTB assists the USTR in the worldwide expansion of market access for U.S. goods and services, participates in trade-related intellectual property protection issues, and assists in the negotiation of bilateral and multilateral free trade agreement issues related to wine and spirits.

- **Federal Trade Commission (FTC).** The FTC and TTB have cross-jurisdictional authority in the area of beverage alcohol advertising. TTB has worked with the FTC on several occasions in response to complaints about alcohol advertisements. TTB plans to expand its Advertising Enforcement Program, which will provide ample opportunities for working together with the FTC.

- **Federation of Tax Administrators (FTA).** The FTA represents State agencies that collect taxes. TTB attends FTA meetings that focus on the collection of excise taxes on alcohol and tobacco products. During these meetings, TTB and representatives of the various State agencies share information and foster relationships to improve efforts on the Federal and State levels to collect excise taxes that are rightfully due.

- **National Association of State Attorneys General (NAAG).** NAAG is the coordinator of the Master Settlement Agreements (MSA) concerning cigarettes and smokeless tobacco among the various State governments. Because NAAG is interested in collecting MSA payments from domestic manufacturers and importers, TTB has provided domestic production and import information to NAAG, in accordance with the provisions of the IRC. TTB continues to offer assistance and provide information to NAAG and the State governments.

TTB will seek areas of similar activity, so that measures of performance can be compared across agencies.

APPENDIX D: Program Evaluations

TTB uses internal and external program evaluations to validate performance measures, determine the effectiveness of our programs.

Internal TTB Program Evaluations

The following TTB Internal program evaluations have been completed or are currently in progress at the time of this writing:

- Puerto Rico Operations,

- Tax Collection Activities, and

- American Viticultural Areas.

Program Evaluations currently in process are:

- Exports Verification (report writing stage), and

- Adverse Actions (conducting field work)

- Review of contractor recommendations listed below for "TTB Protect the Public Business Process Reengineering Study" (2005-2006).

External TTB Program Evaluations

The following external program evaluations and reviews have been completed:

- TTB commissioned a contractor to perform a "National Revenue Center (NRC) Process Reengineering Study" that resulted in NRC's major reorganization into mission areas for Collect the Revenue and Protect the Public (Completed June 2004).

- TTB underwent a Program Assessment Rating Tool Review (PART) for the Collect the Revenue mission in FY 2005 and received an Effective (Highest) rating (Spring/Summer 2005).

- Office of Inspector General (OIG) reviewed TTB's ability to break away from ATF's ITD infrastructure and the risk model used for audit selection (2005).

- TTB commissioned an 8-A contractor to perform a "TTB Protect the Public Business Process Reengineering Study" (2005-2006).

In addition to various program evaluations, customer surveys gauge program impact and customer satisfaction with TTB services provided to industry and Government.

TTB expects this level of program oversight and evaluation to continue through FY 2012 and beyond. The Bureau also conducts periodic program and office reviews, which cover areas such as personnel, training, office security, quality, and quantity of investigations and audits, and internal controls.

APPENDIX E: Environmental Assessment

TTB will use the American Customer Satisfaction Index (ACSI) Web survey for several programs to determine how well TTB meets the needs of our industry customers. Using the ACSI survey also allows TTB to benchmark against the best in business and Government. TTB intends to conduct focus groups with industry partners to assess what is needed to fully implement electronic Government.

Triennial office reviews performed by TTB will include analysis of employee and customer satisfaction. TTB conducts employee satisfaction surveys through the Federal Human Capital Survey. At the time of this writing, the Treasury Department was constructing a Treasury-wide Human Capital Survey.

TTB will evaluate and compile pertinent demographic, social, and other environmental information. TTB will evaluate and use all of these elements to underpin the development of TTB's Strategic Plan.

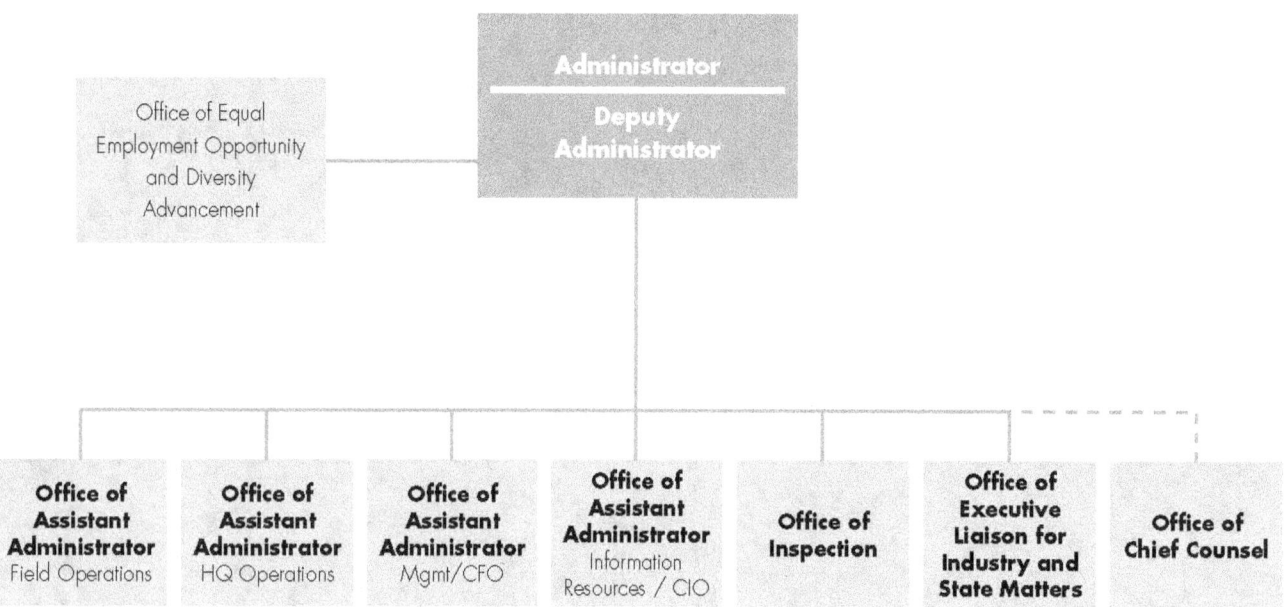

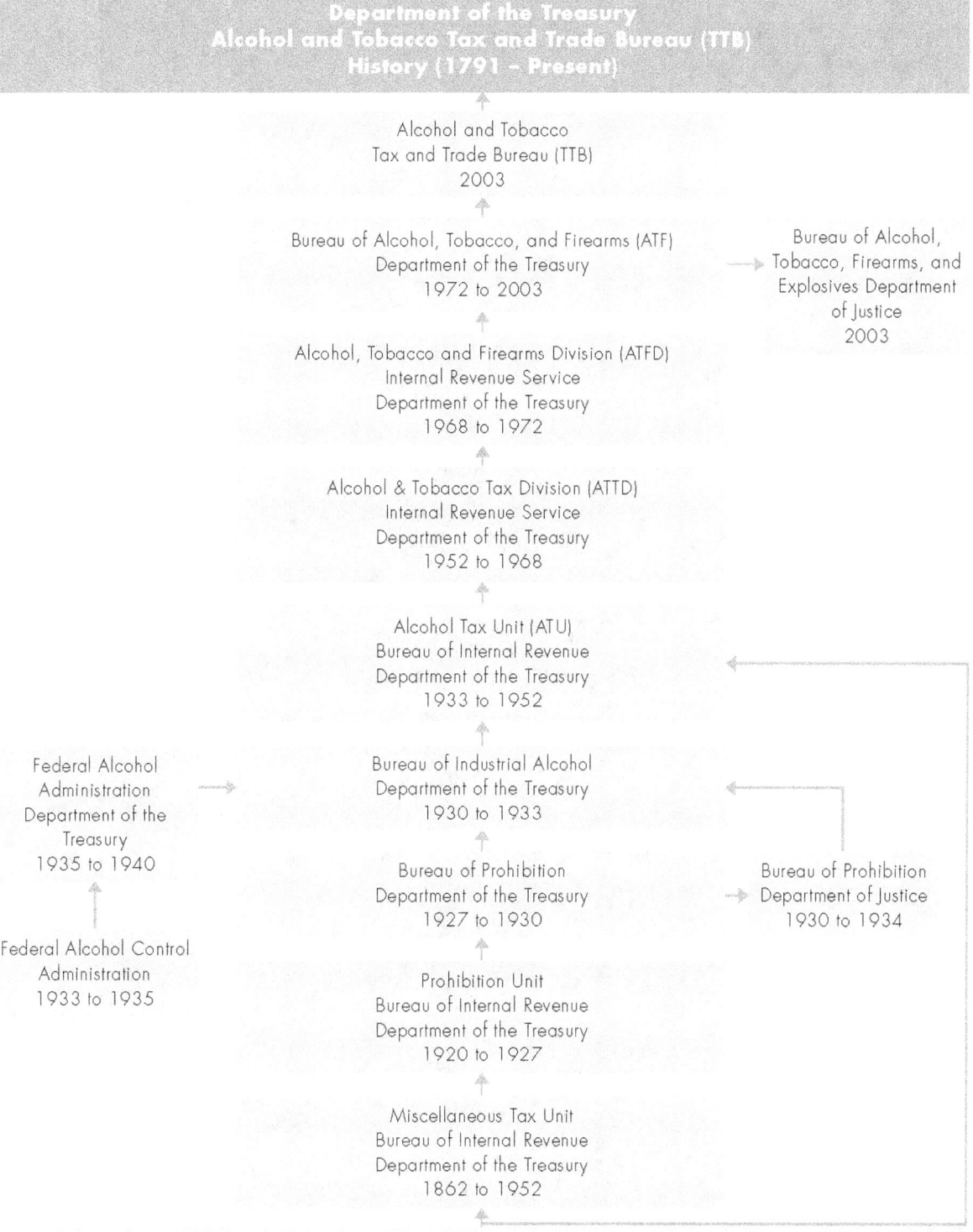

Department of the Treasury
Alcohol and Tobacco Tax and Trade Bureau (TTB)
History (1791 – Present)

Alcohol and Tobacco
Tax and Trade Bureau (TTB)
2003

Bureau of Alcohol, Tobacco, and Firearms (ATF)
Department of the Treasury
1972 to 2003

Bureau of Alcohol, Tobacco, Firearms, and Explosives Department of Justice
2003

Alcohol, Tobacco and Firearms Division (ATFD)
Internal Revenue Service
Department of the Treasury
1968 to 1972

Alcohol & Tobacco Tax Division (ATTD)
Internal Revenue Service
Department of the Treasury
1952 to 1968

Alcohol Tax Unit (ATU)
Bureau of Internal Revenue
Department of the Treasury
1933 to 1952

Federal Alcohol
Administration
Department of the
Treasury
1935 to 1940

Bureau of Industrial Alcohol
Department of the Treasury
1930 to 1933

Bureau of Prohibition
Department of the Treasury
1927 to 1930

Bureau of Prohibition
Department of Justice
1930 to 1934

Federal Alcohol Control
Administration
1933 to 1935

Prohibition Unit
Bureau of Internal Revenue
Department of the Treasury
1920 to 1927

Miscellaneous Tax Unit
Bureau of Internal Revenue
Department of the Treasury
1862 to 1952

The United States Department of the Treasury and the first Federal taxes on distilled spirits were established in 1791.

For additional information regarding the TTB Strategic Plan, please contact:

Alcohol and Tobacco Tax and Trade Bureau
1310 G Street NW., Suite 300 East
Washington, DC 20220

Phone: 202-927-5000
E-mail: ttbquestions@ttb.gov

Visit us on the Web at www.TTB.gov.

TTB P 1995.05 (09/2008)

www.ingramcontent.com/pod-product-compliance
Lightning Source LLC
Chambersburg PA
CBHW080609290526
45790CB00007B/2702